W9-ANU-823

Things to Make and Do

Things to Make and Do

Carol Deacon

p

This is a Parragon Publishing Book

This edition published in 2004

Parragon Publishing
Queen Street House
4 Queen Street
Bath BA1 IHE, UK

Copyright © Parragon 2002

Designed, produced, and packaged by Stonecastle Graphics Limited

Text by Carol Deacon
Craft items by Carol Deacon
Edited by Gillian Haslam
Designed by Sue Pressley and Paul Turner
Photography by Roddy Paine

All rights reserved. No part of this publication may be reproduced,
stored in a retrieval system, or transmitted in any way or by any
means, electronic, mechanical, photocopying, recording, or otherwise,
without the prior permission of the copyright holder.

ISBN 1-40540-412-4

Printed in China

Contents

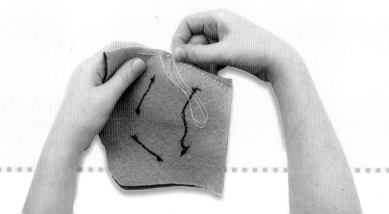

Introduction

This book is intended
to give you lots of ideas for things to
make for yourself and also as gifts for others.
However, there are a few ground rules that you need
to follow if you're not going to get into trouble!

1 Never wear your
best clothes when
you're doing craftwork.
Always wear an
apron or old
clothes.

2 When using paints, glue, or anything messy,
always put down newspaper first to protect
the table.

3 Always make
sure that you've got
everything you need before you start and
read the instructions all the way through
before you begin. If there's anything you
don't understand - ask!

4 If you're using
spray paint,
spray outside. Use plenty
of newspaper and a mask
too, as it is important that
you don't inhale the paint.

5 If you're decorating items of clothing, ask first. Don't borrow someone's favorite jeans and decorate them without their permission. They may not be as pleased as you think!

6 And finally – always, always, always, clean up after you've finished. Then mom will be happy and when you ask if you can make something again on another day, she'll say "Of course you can!".

Have fun!

Carol Deacon

Decorated Boxes

Decorated boxes are easy to make and make lovely gifts. I bought these inexpensive undecorated ones from a craft store. However, you could always make your own or paint and decorate an empty box you already have at home.

These two boxes were painted first, then decorated with beads, glass pebbles, ribbons, and stickers.

This box was tied with a piece of raffia (you could also use string if you like,) then some paper roses were pushed under the knot.

To make your box

You will need:
- Box
- Paints (if painting)
- Decorations (beads, shells, flowers, ribbon etc)
- Glue
- Scissors if you need to cut ribbon

1 Paint the box if you wish and leave it to dry.

2 Place the decorations in position and glue them in place.

This purple rose box looks very impressive but in fact I used a Christmas table decoration and stuck it on the top with double-sided tape. The decoration was so grand the box didn't need anything else!

Tortoise String Holder

He's not only handsome to look at, he's extremely useful too. You'll never wonder where the string is again with this chap looking after it!

To make your tortoise string holder

You will need:

- Plastic margarine tub
- Ping pong ball
- Green spray or oil-based model paint
- Paintbrush
- Cardboard egg box
- Scissors
- String
- Googly eyes (optional)
- Black permanent felt tip pen
- Glue
- Sticky stars

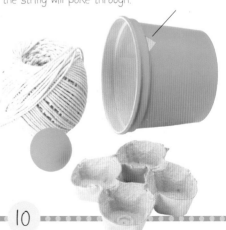

1 Cut a small triangular hole out of the side of a margarine tub. This is where the string will poke through.

2 Paint or spray the top and base of the margarine tub green and allow to dry. Also paint the ping pong ball.

3 Cut a section of four egg holders from of a cardboard egg box. Trim the top to make it flat and also paint green. Leave it to dry and then stick it to the margarine tub lid.

4 To attach the head to the body, use a pair of scissors or a cake skewer. CAREFULLY make two holes into the ping pong ball and the front of the painted margarine tub.

5 Push a short length of string through the two holes in the ball. Then thread the two ends of string through the two holes in the margarine tub. Tie the ends in a knot inside the tub.

6 Stick the eyes onto the head and draw a mouth using the pen.

7 Place the ball of string inside the tortoise's shell and poke the end of the string through the hole in the side of the tub.

8 Finish off by decorating the tortoise's shell with stick-on stars.

Tip
You may find a green colored ping pong ball at a sports store.

Twig Picture Frames

The next time you go for a walk in the woods, bring back a few twigs. With a little imagination they can be turned into picture frames which make lovely gifts for birthdays or Christmas.

Thicker pieces of wood also work well.

To make your frame:

You will need:

- Four twigs
- Photo or picture
- Scissors
- Thick cardboard
- Double-sided tape
- Skewer or knitting needle
- Glue suitable for wood and paper
- String or raffia

1 Decide what you want to frame and cut out a section from a large cardboard box to the size you want.

2 Stick the picture or photograph onto the cardboard with a little double-sided tape.

3 Make a hole through the picture with a skewer or knitting needle. Thread the string through one of the holes to leave a loop. Tie a knot at the end.

4 Push the string through the other hole and tie another knot. Snip the end of the strings to neaten them.

5 Cut the bits of twig to size. Stick them around the edges with glue and leave the frame to dry.

You could spray the twigs first with silver or gold spray paint.

Pencil Holders

Stop people pinching your pencils by storing them in an elegant pencil holder. Although as it's so nice, you might have to be wary about people pinching the pencil holder instead!

To make your pencil holder

You will need:

- An aluminum food tin
- Decorations such as glass pebbles, shells, feathers, fake jewels, and gems, etc.
- Strong glue
- Raffia (available from craft and garden centers)
- Scissors

Tip

Some can openers remove the entire top of the can leaving a top edge that is extremely sharp and dangerous. Avoid cans opened like this and use a can opener that cuts just inside the top edge or one that opens with a ring pull.

14

Variations:

Spread glue over the outside of the can and wind string around the can. (The hairy sort of string is best!) Use another two strands of string to tie into a bow to finish it off. Or spread glue over the outside of the can and cover with denim or other fabric. Finish off with a big bright ribbon tied in a bow. Or glue on a scrap of fabric and finish off with a ribbon tied in a big, bright bow. This denim covered can has a great frayed edge which is very effective but easy to create.

1 Carefully wash and dry a metal food can.

2 Glue the glass pebbles around the sides of the tin. Leave it to dry.

3 Tie a few strands of raffia around the top of the can in a bow.

Splatter Vest Top

In the summertime you can buy little tops like these very cheaply. It's easy then to customize them to make them look exclusive!

You will need:

• Vest top

• Plastic bag

• Newspaper

• 2-3 pots fabric paint

(in the color or colors of your choice!)*

• Large, soft paintbrush

• A few sheets of absorbent kitchen paper

Important: Read the instructions on the fabric paint bottles in case they differ from the ones given here.

To make your splatter vest top:

1 Place the plastic bag flat inside the vest. This will help to stop the dye soaking through the fabric and spoiling the back of the vest.

Tip
You could also use glitter fabric paints. Apply them after fixing the dye.

2 Place the vest and bag onto newspaper.

3 Dip the brush into the first pot of dye and flick or splatter it over the vest.

4 If you're using more than one color, rinse the brush and dry it on some kitchen paper.

6 Leave the vest to dry, then fix the color by covering it with a clean cloth and ironing on a hot heat for a couple of minutes.

5 Repeat the flicking and splattering with the rest of the colors.

Squishy Squashy Bean Bags

Bean bags are easy to make and fun to play with. You can decorate them in all sorts of ways. I've used felt for these as it doesn't fray at the edges which makes it easy to use.

To make a squishy squashy bean bag

1 Cut out two irregular squarish pieces of felt.

You will need:

• Brown, white and black felt (though you can vary this depending upon your design)
• Pins
• Scissors
• Black thread and needle
• Glue
• Black felt pen (optional)
• About 6oz dried beans, lentils or split peas

2 Cut out two white felt circles for the eyes and two smaller black ones for the pupils.

3 Cut out a larger brown circle then cut this in half to make two eyelids.

4 Place one black circle onto a white one and stitch onto one of the big pieces of felt using black thread. Just stitch over the same spot two or three times to hold it in place. If you really can't sew, then glue it instead! Repeat with the other eye.

5 Position the eyelids and stitch along the edge of the eyelid with a line of backstitch. You can cheat and glue these on instead if you want.

6 To make his mouth, sew a wavy backstitched line along the lower part of his face. For quicker results, you could draw a line with a black felt tip pen instead.

7 Turn the face over and place it on top of the other big piece of felt. With the face facing inward, backstitch around the outside edge of the bag. Leave the bottom of the bag open.

8 Turn the bag the right way out and tip some lentils or dried beans into the bag. Don't fill it too full or it won't be able to squish!

9 Overstitch along the base of the bag to close it. Use fairly small close together stitches to stop your beans falling out.

Crafty Cook

A great present for someone who likes to cook! Be careful using the cheese grater because it's very sharp in places.

How to make a crafty cook

You will need:
- Wooden spoon
- Pastry brush
- Sticky tape
- Black food color pen (available from kitchen or cake decorating stores)
- Cheese grater
- Kitchen paper
- Pastry cutter
- Lemon juicer
- 39in ribbon
- Scissors

1 Tape the spoon and brush together with sticky tape.

2 Draw the face on the spoon with the food color pen.

3 Stand the grater upright and stuff with kitchen paper.

4 Push the spoon and brush down inside the back of the grater.

5 Push the handles of the cutter and juicer into the front so that they stand out like arms.

6 Tie the ribbon in a neat bow around the spoon and shape the ends.

Tip

If you don't want to use a lemon squeezer and pastry cutter, choose spoons or other kitchen things instead.

Decorated Notebooks

Personalize and decorate a plain notebook quickly and easily. A great gift idea for a special friend or simply something stylish to scribble your secrets in.

To decorate your notebook

You will need:
- Plain notebook
- Glue
- Scissors
- 30cm (12in) ribbon per book
- Stuff for decorating your book – glitter, feathers, pictures, etc.

1 To make a glitter heart like the one pictured above, spread glue into a heart shape on the front cover. Sprinkle with red glitter, then tip the excess away.

2 Make a glue wiggly line around the heart and sprinkle with silver glitter. Tip the excess away.

3 To attach the ribbon, cut two 6in lengths of ribbon. Stick one piece inside the front cover and one inside the back. Leave to dry, then tie together to close the book.

Tip

If you want to stop the glitter from falling off once the glue has dried, cut a square from a clear plastic food bag and stick over the top. Use strips of clear sticky tape around the edges. A square of clear sticky-backed plastic would also work.

Variations

Feathers also make an excellent and unusual decoration. You can buy colored ones from craft or notions stores. But let's not stop there! You could decorate your notebooks with all sorts of other things – photographs, pictures cut out of magazines, stick-on stars – anything that's flat and takes your fancy!

Sliced Jelly Oranges

Apparently my grandma used to make these jelly oranges as treats for my mother on her birthday. Save the juice as you squeeze the oranges – you really can't beat real freshly squeezed juice.

To make the sliced jelly oranges

You will need:

• 4-6 oranges (each one makes four slices so use as many as you need.)
• Sharp knife
• Orange juice squeezer
• Jug for collecting juice
• Spoon
• 2-3 different packets of jelly
• Shallow dish

1 Wash and dry the oranges.

2 Cut the oranges in half and squeeze out the juice. Then scoop out the centers.

3 Make up the jelly mixtures as directed on the packets.

4 Stand the orange halves in a shallow dish so that they cannot wobble about too much once they are filled.

5 Pour the jelly carefully into each orange half.

Tip

If you're using different flavors of jelly, you may not need to use each entire packet. Just use half and halve the amount of water needed.

6 Leave to set in the refrigerator overnight.

7 When required, remove from the refrigerator and slice each half into quarters.

Hanging Shelf Frogs

This is a really easy way to bring a bit of humor into your room. These frogs have extra long arms which, if you bend them over along the dotted lines, can hook over the edges of shelves in your room. If you stand a book or something heavy on the flap to stop them blowing away, they'll hang about quite happily!

To make your hanging shelf frogs

You will need:

- Pencil
- Tracing or greaseproof paper
- Green cardboard
- Black marker pen
- Scissors

1 Trace over these frog templates using the tracing paper and pencil. If you want the frogs to be bigger, you could enlarge them using a photocopier.

2 Turn the tracing paper over and re-draw over the outlines on the wrong side of the paper.

3 Place the tracing paper, right way up, onto the green cardboard and draw over the outline a third time. The image in pencil should now be lightly visible on the green card.

4 Draw over the outline on the green cardboard using the black marker pen.

5 Carefully cut around the outside of the outline with scissors.

6 Bend the arms along the dotted lines and hook over a shelf!

Of course you needn't stop at frogs. You can use this long arm trick to draw and hang other creatures from your shelves.

How many more shelf hangers can you design?

Height Chart

Check that you're still growing with a handy height chart. You could put measurements on the chart too. If you do, be sure that you hang the chart the right height off the ground.

To make your height chart

You will need:
• A piece of colored cardboard about 24in x 8in (you could make it longer if you like by sticking two pieces together)
• Ruler
• Black marker pen
• Paints or crayons
• Hole punch (optional)
• String (optional)

64
62
60
58
56
54
52
50
48
46
44
42

1 Draw a line down the center of the cardboard using the ruler and the pen.

2 Make marks if you wish at 2in intervals.

3 Draw the outline of the pattern on one side of the chart.

4 Fill in the outlines with your paints or crayons.

5 When the paint has dried, cut two holes in the top. Either use a hole punch or make holes with a pair of scissors. Thread string through the holes and knot at the back. Alternatively, you could leave the holes out completely and just attach the chart to the wall with blu-tack.

Tip
You could stick pictures cut out of magazines or even pictures of members of the family down the side of the chart instead.

150

145

140

135

130

Personalized Place Mats

Not only a great way to show off your artistic talent, but a useful gift too! It's fun to draw a portrait of each member of the family but you could sketch anything you want.

To make your personalized place mats

You will need:
- 1 sheet paper or cardboard per place mat
- Crayons or paints
- Clear sticky-backed plastic
- Sharp scissors

1 Draw your designs onto the sheets of paper.

2 Leaving the backing paper in place, cut out two sticky backed plastic rectangles. They should be about $1/2$in bigger all round than the paper.

3 Partially peel away some of the backing paper from one of the sticky-backed plastic rectangles. Place the drawing face down onto the sticky side and pull the rest of the backing away.

4 Smooth the plastic covering over the picture then repeat on the back.

5 Trim around the edges of the mat to neaten them. Leave about a 1/4in border around the edges.

Tip

For a really professional finish, you could have your drawings laminated at a stationers.

Miniature Garden

Miniature gardens are great fun to make. This one is fairly simple but you could also use twigs to make trees, moss to make grass, stones to make a rockery, and even a sunken lid to make a pond.

Little toadstools made out of modeling clay will give your garden a magical feel. You could also add small toys or animals. Remember, though, that plants are living things so treat them carefully and water them lightly but regularly. If they get too big for your garden, be kind and replant them in something bigger.

You will need:
- A shallow dish or watertight tray. Foil food trays or containers are also ideal.
- A few handfuls of gravel
- A few handfuls of potting compost or soil
- Assorted small plants – heather, spider plants, moss etc
- Decoration such as shells, small pebbles, twigs, toys, play sand
- Modeling clay (if you want to make toadstools or gnomes)

To make your miniature garden

1 Place a layer of gravel in the base of the dish to provide a little drainage.

2 Place a layer of potting compost or soil on top.

3 To make a path in your garden, dig a small trench and fill with more gravel, pebbles or play sand.

4 Dig small holes and plant your plants.

Variation

For a simple yet effective gift, place a terra-cotta flowerpot on its side. Use bits of modeling clay to keep it steady. Place a tiny plant in a tiny flowerpot inside (you can keep this in place with a bit of modeling clay). Make a tiny gnome out of modelling clay if you wish and place him by the side of the flowerpot. Scatter a little gravel inside the main pot.

5 Edge your borders with a line of small shells or pebbles.

6 Make and add toadstools, gnomes, or toys if you wish.

Hanging Pictures

This would make a lovely gift for Mothering Sunday. I used fabric flowers which stuck quite easily with a blob of glue. You could also use it to frame pictures or family photographs instead.

To make your hanging pictures

You will need:

- 6 pieces of cardboard about 6 x 5in
- Ruler
- Pencil
- Craft knife
- Glue in tube with pointed nozzle
- Pictures or flowers to go into frames
- Gold spray paint
- Knitting needle or skewer
- Curling parcel ribbon

1 Cut a window out of three of the pieces of cardboard.

2 Pipe a squiggly line or lines of glue around the edge of the frame. Leave to dry overnight.

3 When the glue is dry, spray the whole frame with the gold paint.

4 If using pictures, stick them to the back pieces of cardboard now. Then stick the gold frame on top.

5 If you're using flowers, stick the frames together and stick the flowers on afterward.

6 Make two holes top and bottom in two of the frames using a skewer or knitting needle. Make only two holes on the top edge of the bottom picture.

7 Starting with the bottom frame, push a long length of curling ribbon through the hole and tie a knot at the back. Thread the ribbon into and behind the other two frames, leaving a loop at the top for hanging.

8 Tie a knot where the ribbon comes back into the bottom frame and cut off any excess.

Decorated Jeans

These wonderful glitter fabric paints come in tubes which you simply squeeze onto the fabric to make patterns. If you rub a drop into the denim, you get a sparkly patch. Never has updating jeans been so easy!

To decorate your jeans

You will need:
• 1 pair clean, dry jeans (Check first that it's okay to use them!)
• Glitter fabric paints

1 Decorate one side at a time and allow it to dry before decorating the other side.

2 Place the jeans flat on some newspaper and squeeze the fabric paints onto the jeans. Spirals are an easy yet trendy shape to do.

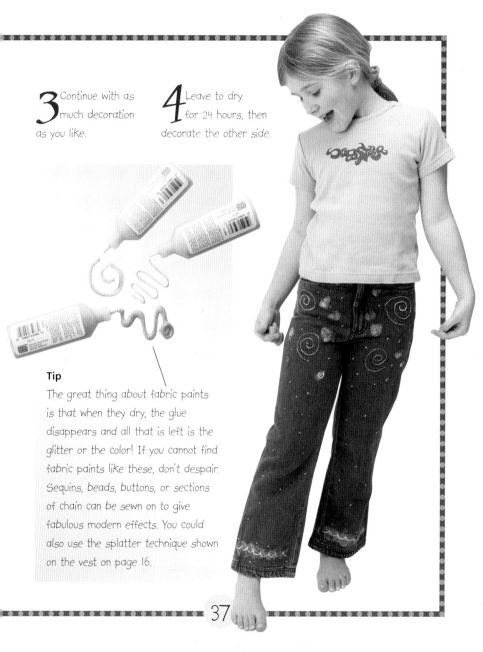

3 Continue with as much decoration as you like.

4 Leave to dry for 24 hours, then decorate the other side.

Tip

The great thing about fabric paints is that when they dry, the glue disappears and all that is left is the glitter or the color! If you cannot find fabric paints like these, don't despair. Sequins, beads, buttons, or sections of chain can be sewn on to give fabulous modern effects. You could also use the splatter technique shown on the vest on page 16.

Printed Wrapping Paper

This stylish wrapping paper is decorated with your own unique designs. If you're feeling really crafty, you could team it up with the gift tags on page 42.

To make your wrapping paper

You will need:

- Corrugated cardboard box
- Scissors or craft knife
- Glue
- String
- Acrylic paints
- Newspaper
- Sheets of paper for printing on

1 To make the stampers, cut two or three 4in squares from a corrugated cardboard box.

2 Drizzle a little glue in a spiral shape onto one of the pieces of card.

3 Stick a length of string onto the glue, following the spiral pattern. If the string's too long, trim off the end. Make two or three stampers (depending upon how many colors you plan to use) and leave them to dry for a few hours.

4 When you are ready to print, place a sheet of paper on some newspaper.

5 Dab the paint onto the string using a paintbrush.

6 Press the stamper on to the paper in a random pattern. Repeat using the other stampers and colors.

Gift Bags

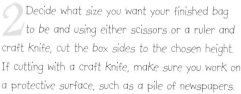

Have you ever looked at those
fancy present bags in the stores
and thought how nice they
looked? Well, here's how to turn a humble
cereal packet into an elegant gift bag in no time at all!

To make your gift bags

You will need:
- Cardboard food packets (e.g. small cereal or ice-cream cone packets)
- Scissors or ruler and craft knife
- Glue
- Sticky tape
- Hole punch (optional)
- Cans of spray paint or paint such as acrylic or poster paint
- Ribbon or string for handles (you'll need about 16in per bag)

1 Undo the flaps on both the top and bottom of the packet and flatten it.

2 Decide what size you want your finished bag to be and using either scissors or a ruler and craft knife, cut the box sides to the chosen height. If cutting with a craft knife, make sure you work on a protective surface, such as a pile of newspapers.

3 If you plan to spray your bag, you can leave it like this and just use glue or sticky tape to re-close the bottom. If you are going to paint it, you will need to slit open the glued side fastening and turn the bag inside out. This will give you a cardboard surface suitable for painting on. Re-fasten the seam and bottom of the bag.

4 Use the hole puncher to cut two holes on each side of the bag ready for the handles. If you don't have a hole punch, carefully make holes using the point of a pair of scissors.

5 Spray or paint your bag. Be as creative as you like. Flowery or swirly patterns would also look great.

6 When the bag is dry, thread about 8in of ribbon or string through the holes to make the handles. Tie a knot inside the bag to hold the handles in place.

Tip

For even grander designs, you could add feathers, glitter, and silver or gold stick-on stars.

Gift Tags

These easy-to-make gift tags will add a bit of magic to your presents. They would also look good attached to the gift bags on page 40.

To make your gift tags

You will need:
- Colored cardboard cut into rectangles about 5¹/₂in x 4in
- Scissors or craft knife
- Hole punch
- Ribbon (about 16in) per gift tag
- Curling parcel ribbon

1 Fold the piece of cardboard in half then open it flat.

2 Cut two diagonal slits through the front of the card.

3 Thread the ribbon through the slits so that the long ends are pulled through the front.

4 Tie the ribbon into a bow and trim the ends if necessary.

Tip

If you don't want to make holes in your tags, you could attach them to your presents with double-sided tape instead.

5 Cut a hole through the top corner of the gift tag with the hole punch

6 Thread a length of curling ribbon through the hole.

7 Write your message and tie onto your parcel.

Glove Puppet

You know when you lose a glove and mom looks a bit annoyed and says what on earth is the use of one glove? Well, now you can tell her that one glove is exactly what you need to make this glove puppet. You can make whatever characters you like. You could even write a short play for them to perform!

To make your glove puppet

You will need:
- A glove
- Five absorbent cotton balls
- Black thread
- Decorations: googly eyes, sparkly shapes, bits of ribbon and yarn, feathers, lace, pipecleaner etc.
- Glue
- Scissors
- Black felt tip pen

1 To make a head, stuff a ball of absorbent cotton right to the end of each finger. Wrap a length of thread a few times tightly beneath the head and tie in a knot.

2 Decorate each finger. It's fun to make each finger a different character. You can stick bits of braided yarn or strands of embroidery floss on some of the heads for hair.

3 You can either use stick-on eyes or glue circles of white paper on the heads for eyes, then add black felt tip dots for pupils.

4 Sparkly shapes also make great decorations. Heart or half moon shapes can be used to make mouths. You can also sew mouth and nose shapes using a little black thread.

5 For the baby, a little piece of yarn was threaded through a short bit of lace using a simple running stitch. Then the yarn was pulled tight so that the lace ruffled up slightly. It was stuck onto the baby's head and the yarn tied into a bow beneath his chin.

6 A bit of pipe cleaner was used to make the Indian's headdress. The ends were twisted together behind the head and a feather stuck down the back.

Cellphone Pouch

This would make a great present for anyone who can't move without their cellphone! The furry fabric is fun and colorful, but you could also use fake leather fabric if you prefer.

To make your cellphone pouch

1 Measure the length of the phone (minus the antennae) and cut out a strip of fabric 2½ times the length of the phone and about 4in wide.

You will need:

- Tape measure or ruler
- Furry fabric
- Sharp scissors
- Needle and thread

Tip
If you use fabric that doesn't fray, you won't need to hem the edges.

2 Cut the corners off one end to make the flap a rounded shape.

3 Fold the fabric with the right side on the inside. Pin the sides together so that the rounded end forms a flap.

4 Using backstitch, sew along the two long sides.

5 If you want to attach it to a belt, cut two slits into the back of the holder. Oversew (this means you sew over the same spot over and over again using one stitch) the two ends of each slit to stop the fabric pulling and stretching.

6 Turn the holder the right way and slot onto your belt.

Fancy Napkin Rings

These are so easy to make and would look lovely on the table at Christmas.

To make a fancy napkin ring

You will need:
• 2-3 cardboard kitchen roll centers (please don't use toilet roll centers – they're not very hygienic!)
• Ruler
• Scissors
• Gold and/or silver spray

1 Cut about a 3in long section off a kitchen roll tube.

Tip

If you wish, you could always paint the napkin rings with acrylic paints instead. Why not stick bits of tinsel on for extra sparkle!

3 When you have finished, pull the spiral apart slightly and place to one side. Make the rest of the napkin rings.

2 Hold the scissors at a slight angle and cut around the tube. You should see the spiral shape starting to form almost immediately.

4 When you've made enough napkin rings, place them on a piece of newspaper and spray them gold or silver.

T-Shirt Pillows

Have you ever had a favorite T-shirt that you've grown out of but can't bear to throw away? Now you can give it a new lease of life and change it into a pillow!

To make your pillow

You will need:

- T shirt
- Yarn
- Darning needle
- Scissors
- Batting
- Decoration for T shirt if required

Tip

To make a similar pillow
for a boy, either use a
more masculine colored
T-shirt or stuff a
baseball shirt instead.

1 Thread some yarn onto the needle and tie a knot in the end.

2 Using a very simple running stitch, sew along one of the armholes to close it.

3 Sew around the other armhole and the neck hole as well.

4 Stuff the pillow Sew a final line of running stitch or blanket stitch along the bottom of the T-shirt to close it.

5 If there's no printed pattern on your T-shirt and you feel it's a bit plain, stick some felt shapes onto the front of the cushion or draw on a pattern using fabric paints.

Braided Picture Frame

Braiding is a very ancient craft and very easy to do. Once you've mastered the art, you can braid all sorts of things – string, grass, ribbon, even your friend's hair!

To make your braided picture frame

You will need:

• 3 sheets of colored paper
• Stapler
• Picture or photograph
• Pieces of cardboard
• Glue
• Scissors

1 Cut the colored paper into thin strips about ¼in wide. You will need three strips of different colors per side.

2 Staple the three strips together at the top. This will hold them together while you're braiding.

3 Start to plait. To do this, take an outside strip and fold it across the middle one. Then take the strip furthest away on the other side and fold it across the middle strip. Make four plaited strips – one for each side.

4 Stick your picture or photograph onto a piece of cardboard.

5 Cut the braided strips to size and stick around the picture to form a frame.

6 To make a freestanding picture, cut out a cardboard triangle. Fold and bend one side and stick onto the back of the picture with sticky tape.

7 Alternatively you could stick it on the wall with blu-tack or make two holes in the top and thread some string through.

Tip

Stick a small paper calendar (available from stationers) on the bottom and you've got a great Christmas present for someone.

Life-Size Self-Portrait

A roll of lining paper from the do-it-yourself store is not only cheap but will provide you with an almost endless supply of drawing paper! Hang your portrait on the wall when you've finished and stand next to it occasionally to check that you're still growing!

How to make your life-size self-portrait

You will need:

- Newspaper
- About 60in lining paper (depending upon how tall you are)
- 1 extra person to draw around you!
- Black marker pen
- Paints and crayons

1 Place some newspaper on the floor and lay your sheet of lining paper on top.

2 Lie on top of the paper and get someone to draw around you using the marker pen.

Tip

If the paper keeps curling up, roll it up the other way to the way it wants to go. Un-roll it and it should now lie flat. You can also place heavy objects on the corners to hold it in place.

3 Fill in the outline with your paints and crayons. Be as creative as you like.

Trinket Box

A special little box for storing all your little treasures. It would make a nice present for someone too!

To make your trinket box

You will need:

• 32 popsicle sticks (packs can be bought from kitchen equipment or craft stores)

• Glue suitable for sticking wood

• Scissors

• 1 square of felt

• Paint or spray for decoration

• Tissue paper for lining the box.

1 Stick about twelve popsicle sticks together to form the base of the box.

2 Measure and cut a square of felt slightly smaller than the base you've just made. Glue this onto the popsicle stick base.

3 To make the sides, use four sticks per side and stick together. Glue one stick diagonally on top of each section.

4 Leave all the sections to dry for a few hours.

5 When they're dry, glue all the sections together and leave to dry overnight.

6 When the glue is dry, you can paint your box if you wish. It can also be sprayed silver or gold or left plain and natural.

Tip
For a really glamorous finish you could also glue on feathers, tinsel, or plastic "jewels."

Decorated Bulletin Board

This is an easy way to brighten up a dull bulletin board. Choose colors to match the color theme in your bedroom.

To decorate your bulletin board

You will need:

- A cork bulletin board
- Thin colored cardboard in three colors
- Black felt pen
- Scissors
- Craft glue

1 Draw a number of simple faces on to the pieces of cardboard. Make sure you leave a bit of space around them for cutting them out.

2 Cut each one into a simple irregular shape. You will need about 27 shapes for a 16in × 12in board. Make more if necessary.

3 Arrange the shapes around the board. You can either do this randomly or in a pattern — green, purple, blue, green, purple, blue, etc. Glue the faces into position.

Copy these faces or design some of your own.

Hobby Horse

A hobby horse is a wonderful toy. Not only can you win races with it but you can also use it to ride around the yard. Why not get your friends to make one too then you can all go out for rides together.

To make your hobby horse

You will need:

- 1 sock – color and size of your choice!
- Stuffing, batting or bits of old pantyhose or fabric to stuff your horse
- Blue, pink, white, and black felt
- Tracing or greaseproof paper
- Pen
- Scissors
- Glue
- Needle and thread
- Yarn and darning needle
- Broomstick or pole for body
- Sticky tape
- Ribbon (about 6ft)

1 Stuff the sock to make the horse's head shape.

2 Trace the shapes for the eyes and ears from page 64 onto tracing paper or greaseproof paper.

3 Cut out the shapes and draw round them onto the felt. You will need two of each shape.

4 Cut the shapes out of the felt. Stick the eyes onto the head using glue. (Or you can stitch them on if you prefer.) Stick the black pupil onto the white, then stick the blue eyelid over the top.

5 For the ears, place the pink inner section on top of the blue. Fold the two in half and stitch them onto the head. Just sew over the same spot over and over again to hold them in place.

6 To make the mane, thread the darning needle with some yarn. Thread about 4in through the top of the horses head. Cut the yarn leaving a 4in tail as well.

7 Cut the yarn very close to the needle to release it and tie the two ends of yarn into a knot to leave a small fringe. Repeat down the horse's back and over the top of his eyes.

8 Push the stick into the sock and wind tape around the horse's neck to hold it in place and to close the sock.

9 Wind extra ribbon around the tape to hide it and finish him off with a large, smart bow.

Egg Cozies

To make an egg cozy

These chicken and egg cozies will keep your boiled eggs as warm as toast! They would make great Easter presents too!

You will need:
- Template for cozy shape (page 64)
- Paper
- Pen
- Scissors
- Yellow, red, and white felt
- Black thread
- Needle

1 Trace the egg cozy template on page 64 onto a sheet of paper and cut it out.

2 Draw round it using a pen onto a piece of felt. Cut out two pieces of felt per egg cozy.

3 To make the hen, cut out two white felt circles for the eyes, a yellow diamond shape for the beak, and a wiggly comb shape for the top of the head.

4 Stitch the eyes in place using black thread. If you stitch over the same spot over and over again, it will make a black spot that will look like the hen's pupil and also hold the eye in place.

5 Stitch the beak in place using a line using backstitch across the center of the diamond.

6 Place the two pieces of egg cozy together with base of the wiggly top piece inside the egg cozy. Stitch around the edge of the cosy. If you double up the thread and use two strands instead of one, the stitching will stand out more.

Tip

If you really don't like stitching, you could glue the eyes and beak in place instead and use a black pen to make a dot for the pupils and the smile on the egg character.

7 Make the egg character in exactly the same way. Cut out two pieces of felt and cut and stitch two eyes on to the front. Sew a smile underneath the eyes using a curved line of backstitch.

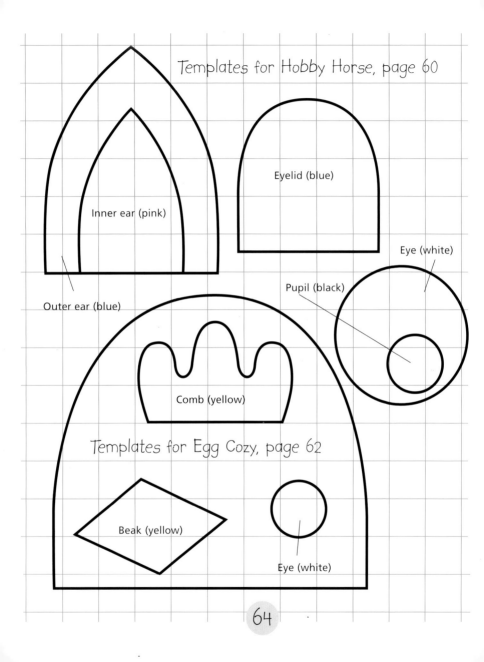

Templates for Hobby Horse, page 60

Inner ear (pink)

Outer ear (blue)

Eyelid (blue)

Eye (white)

Pupil (black)

Comb (yellow)

Templates for Egg Cozy, page 62

Beak (yellow)

Eye (white)